SOUL FOOD

SOUL FOOD

Spiritual Staples for the Journey of Life

Maureene Bass

Valhalla Press
Napa Valley, California

Valhalla Press
P. O. Box 6224
Wine Valley
Napa Valley, California 94581

First Printing
Cover and interior design: Nita Ybarra
Editing: Jennifer Garrett
Linda Altman

Printed in the United States of America

Library of Congress Cataloging in Publication Data
Bass, Maureene
Soul Food
BV4501.2.B38 1996
248.4—dc20
ISBN 0-9645510-0-4

Dedication

To Don Fraser, who saw and held
the vision for me.

To my children, Holly, Blakely, Ellie,
Tim, and Jill, who have always been my most
effective teachers.

To John Rogers who became
an angel before his time.

To John Winston and all others who suffer
the casualties of AIDS.

Contents

Acknowledgments

I acknowledge my gentle and loving guide, the Holy Spirit, who is the undeniable author of this book.

I would also like to thank the "Thursday Morning Voyagers" for their comments as early readers, and a very special thanks to my congregation in Napa Valley who from the onset has held this book in "the Light." Knowledge of the English language, attained from an "old school" foundation made Lora Foote, Runa Schlaffer, and May Chamberlin, invaluable proofreaders. My thanks to you all.

My heartfelt gratitude to Simon Warwick-Smith and Tammy George, who held my hands through this process. All love and thanks to my dear friends Reverend Brent Flecher, Bill Dobbs, and Reverend Pattie Brooks for their faith in me and for practicing their deep spiritual convictions.

My indebtedness goes to Kelly Harrison, my assistant and right hand, for her unwavering support.

I offer my respect and appreciation to those who helped me, directly and indirectly, with the development of this book; and to my many teachers who made sacrifices so that I could learn.

Blessings,
M. B.

Preface

Spiritual Truth is vitally important to every person, for it is the one essential ingredient for living the "good life." The most exalted and profound spiritual knowledge is useless to us until it can be understood, digested, and incorporated into our daily lives. If we are to apply these timeless principles, they must be presented to us in forms that show their practical use.

Soul Food is my attempt to reveal the great Truth Principles in the light, humorous, seemingly unimportant details of ordinary events as they present themselves to us each day. Each morsel presented in this book happened, and illustrates one or more metaphysical truths.

When I began my pursuit for consciousness I read hundreds of personal improvement books. I understood the concepts but could not apply the principles to my personal everyday life. As I continued my search, I turned to philosophy and psychology. It still wasn't enough.

When I returned to the Bible (after a long sabbatical from my intense Christian upbringing), I began to see the Scriptures with new vision. This revised viewpoint came about because of the countless number of inspirational and philosophy books I had ingested and the many religions I had explored during my search.

One basic Truth had repeatedly surfaced in all my studies. This one Truth seemed common to all major religions and philosophies. The more I explored this Truth from various viewpoints, the clearer it became. When my *Aha!* finally arrived I couldn't imagine how I had missed it. But it is hard to find something when it is hidden in plain view—I could not see the forest for the trees.

The elusive, much-sought-after secret is *there is only One Power and One Presence in the universe and that Power is the Omnipresent Godhead. This "hidden" Power is expressed on our plane of existence, through us as our Higher Self or Inner Mind.* From this basic Universal Law all Truth Principles evolve. A review of the teachings of Jesus Christ reveals this truth. He taught that we here on earth receive direct inspiration and can "tune in" through our mind vibration to the one creative Mind of God.

Our subconscious mind is the master of our physical body and the servant of our conscious mind; both the conscious and the subconscious connect us to God Mind. Through our thought vibration we make connection with the Divine Mind and with all phases of human nature.

Proper use of this power begins with the realization that Universal Power flows through each of us as love, harmony, health, peace, joy, right action, abundance, true expression, and inspiration. Unlimited reserve of this power is within each of us, and it can be directed to help us in all our experiences. The Divine Power within us can remove any obstacle; it can overcome any difficulty, be it financial, physical, mental, or spiritual. Proper use of Divine Mind never fails to bring us good.

The simplest entrance into the beneficial flow of this power is through the practice of the Golden Rule—"Do unto others as you would have them do unto you." This is a no-risk action, because we live in a perfectly balanced universe: what goes around, comes around . . . the energy we send to others is the energy we attract . . . like attracts like.

When Truth Principles are discovered and applied, they clear up considerable confusion and make life more manageable. Through taking responsibility for our thoughts and feelings we begin to take charge of our lives as God intended.

Maureene Bass
Napa Valley, California

"It is written, 'Man shall
not live by bread alone . . .' "
Matthew 4:4

Why Wait?

My house is clean; the cat box has fresh litter; my beautiful daughter is coming tonight to spend a few days with me—and I can fit into last year's winter clothes. Life is good.

We frequently miss moments of true happiness because we are waiting for something big to happen before we punch the happiness button. We forget that life is happening while we are waiting. Every moment is a time to cherish our loved ones and to reflect on how good life really is.

Don't Underestimate Yourself

If anyone had said to me, "I bet you can eat a whole cake" I would have laughed and replied, "No way." Yet, on Saturday when I went for a piece of the pineapple upside down cake that I brought home on Tuesday, only a few crumbs remained on the plate. The cake was gone. No one lives with me, so I must have eaten all of it—by myself.

Any task that seems overwhelming usually stops us in our tracks. We forget that any task can be accomplished by breaking it down into do-able parts, or bite-sized pieces.

Just as the cake went down effortlessly, one bite at a time, an enormous project can be successfully executed one task at a time.

Where Are the Angels?

As I look out the airplane window on my way to Washington, D.C., I remember another plane trip 35 years ago, that one from Washington.

I was a flight attendant—stewardess in those days—working a flight from National Airport to Atlanta on a slushy, overcast December day. A little boy going to visit his grandmother was entrusted to my care. He sat very straight in his seat, holding a toy—exactly what, I don't remember. He timidly smiled at me every time I walked by.

Finally he waved me down and asked, "Are we above the clouds yet?" I replied, "Not yet." He stopped me on my return with the same question. Again, I told him, "no" (because the airlines were still flying prop planes in those days, it took longer to reach cruising altitude.)

When we finally slipped through the heavy cloud layer and above the billowy puffs, a breathtaking expanse of blue sky surrounded us. "We are above the clouds now," I told my young passenger.

He peered out the window, then looked back at me with disappointment in his eyes. “Where are the angels?” Thinking quickly, I replied, “Oh! They are out there, we just can’t see them.”

He giggled and pressed his nose against the window for the remainder of the flight.

Ever Changing Reality

Thomas Wolfe was right about going home again. You can't.

When we go home and visit old friends, we view everything from a changed perspective, and thus a changed dimension. Those who have remained at the original locale are still experiencing life from their original viewpoint.

Life is multidimensional. We view it from the dimension available to us at any given time. When we place ourselves in a different location—be it mental, physical, or spiritual—we automatically have access to a new viewpoint. Native Americans have applied this wisdom for centuries: they moved around the medicine wheel knowing that problems are solved when they are viewed from a different position.

Nothing is—or can be—the same when seen from a different viewpoint. Changing your thinking changes your reality.

Play Ball

As children playing baseball, we knew that to get to home plate, we had to round all the bases, touching each one before the umpire called, "You're out."

These simple childhood memories provide two lessons that are valuable to us as adults. One, to advance, we must release the comfortable base of thinking that we have attained. Two, we must hold to a faith that allows us to step off that base with the anticipation of being "safe."

It is physically impossible to advance to a higher step while still clinging to the one below.

I Am Open and Receptive to Change

My move to Napa Valley from Alabama was my opportunity for new and different experiences. Shortly after my arrival in Napa, I ate dinner at a restaurant "up valley" where a friendly waiter recommended the calamari. "Thank you," I said, "but I don't like calamari."

As he walked away I had to admit to myself that I had never tasted calamari. Suddenly I realized that the new experiences I was seeking could be served to me on a silver platter if I was willing to expand my boundaries.

To paraphrase a line from the broadway hit *Auntie Mame*, life is a banquet, and most people are starving to death. Bon Appetit.

Addicted to the Chase

My friend's dog loves to chase balls. The dog and I have a game we play: she drops the ball at my feet, I throw it, she brings it back—and the cycle begins again. She doesn't really want the ball; she just wants to chase it.

How many of us are programmed to chase success? We set an endless series of goals for ourselves, never stopping to enjoy a job well done before we begin the cycle anew. We find it difficult to take the time to bask in any well-earned success. We only look longingly to the next goal that is already in place before we can catch our breath.

If we are addicted to the chase, happiness and contentment will always elude us; the pursuit of success will not bring the fulfillment we are seeking. We can not break the cycle, however, until we realize that the chase itself is the addiction.

"I Feel Like a Good Cry"

The universal symbol of our feeling nature is the heart; yet, as a nation we are so out of touch with these feelings that the term "bleeding heart" is not intended kindly.

As a nation of inventors, we have found a way to experience feelings by proxy: through television and movies we can let actors feel our feelings for us. We can turn on the tube and locate, with our remote control, any emotion of choice—one that we want or need for that particular moment. We can turn on a comedy if we want to be happy, a drama if we want to be sad, and if we are grappling with anger, we can find plenty of violence. We borrow the feelings of the screenwriter as portrayed by the actors. When we have had our fill of any feeling, we cut it off by pushing a button.

We use these methods to get the sensation of the feeling without messy personal entanglements. Could it be a synchronistic connection that we have so many heart bypasses?

Fear of Disclosure

It is said that the eyes are the windows of the soul.

Have you ever noticed how disarming eye-to-eye contact can be? Have you noticed the difficulty that some people have in simply holding your gaze? Could this be caused by a fear of disclosure? Could we have a fear of letting people see our inner truth?

We are afraid that anyone who sees into our soul will know the secret we have been trying to camouflage all our lives. This tenacious secret is the belief that we are not good enough.

We are so busy trying to hide what we think people won't like about us that we forget about our good qualities. When we begin to believe that we are lovable, we advance into a realm of self-acceptance, which invites continual success.

The next time you are afraid to look into someone's eyes, think of one of your lovable qualities and offer it through your eyes. Before you know it, your ego will no longer control the opening to your soul.

As we learn to appreciate our good qualities, we provide an opening for the approval of the world to come flooding in.

Getting Grounded

Yesterday I took my visiting son and daughter-in-law to Calistoga to wallow in the mud baths. It's a wonderful way to get grounded.

It is hard to remember that under the miles and miles of cement that make up our cities and towns, is land—land that is alive and fighting for its survival. When we physically get in touch with nature and actually mix with the dirt that holds this planet together, we connect with a part of the life force that is vital to our spiritual, mental, and physical health.

Because we have covered vast expanses of land with concrete, asphalt, and buildings, many people in urban areas live for extended periods of time totally separated from the healing energies of Mother Earth. Maybe urban dwellers' physical separation from the earth and their inability to receive the healing powers of its life force have a correlation to the escalating crime rate in our cities.

When we love and care for our planet and its life forms, the sanctuary we are creating is for ourselves.

I Do What I Do Because I Want To!

Sometimes we say, "I can't because . . .", or "I wish I could, but I have to . . ." (you fill in the blank). This way of thinking takes away all our power; it establishes us firmly in the position of victim.

Our values determine the decisions we make. We don't "have to do" anything. We could "chuck it all" and head for Timbuktu. Even when the responsibilities and duties we choose to fulfill are not as much fun as something else might be, we need to remember that they are still matters of choice.

It is not the freedom of choice that makes us free, but the realization that everything we do in life is of our own choosing. When we comprehend this, we escape the role of victim, and the door to true freedom and authentic choice swings open.

I make conscious decisions now.

New World

Everything around us is changing. Our attitudes, our way of life, our sources of employment, our support systems—all the things that have been the bedrock of our society—are being transmuted. It is an awesome time in which to live.

It is also a frightening time. We sense that once-solid ground has been replaced with quicksand. It is hard to keep our balance.

The dissolution of our world as we have known it forces us to focus on alternative ways of doing things. This focusing brings a sharpening of our spiritual awareness. We come to understand that we need not fret, for today's world is being replaced by an even grander world of tomorrow.

As we change and grow, we become the major contributors to the transformation of our new world, for our revised attitudes will create the new prevailing standard. Let us commit to growth that transforms our world into one that will make us proud.

Do You Know What Makes You, You?

Our lives sometime resemble a recipe that we make and serve every day. We get tired of the taste of it, but we don't know how to make anything else. For a change, we can serve it on new china, or at another time of day, or with special accouterments, or in candlelight; but it tastes just the same. It doesn't dawn on us that we must change the ingredients of the recipe to get a different taste.

It is madness to do the same thing again and again and expect a different result each time. Yet, it is hard to change our recipe for living if we don't know what ingredients we have been using. Such knowledge comes from introspection, but that is not high on today's list of "most sought after accomplishments."

Over the door of the ancient temples was the phrase "Know Thyself." The wise ones knew that once this was achieved, humankind would be well on its way to a nourishing as well as an exciting life.

"Let There Be Light"

Have you noticed how clothes left hanging in a closet over a period of time shrink? Must be the continual exposure to the dark.

With this realization, I should go into the diet business with a book entitled *The "Stand in the Closet and Let the Dark Shrink You" Diet*. I know it would work, because when we stay in the dark on any subject, we do not grow. When we are close-minded, uninformed, or in the dark, people call us "small." In fact, a sure way not to grow in mind and spirit is to refuse to become enlightened.

It is no coincidence that the symbol for an idea is the light bulb. When we are seeking clarity we sometimes think, "I need to see this in a different light."

As we open to different possibilities and to the dawn of new ideas, people can see our brilliance and they call us "bright."

All new growth and creation begin with the energy vibration we call light.

I Love the Rain

My cat Val acts crazed during long rainy spells. Rain upsets her schedule and keeps her from roaming, and she doesn't like that. One night during a particularly long rainy spell, Val jumped up on me and stomped her feet. After a few meows, I took her to the door. She sat down, looked at the rain, and then looked up at me as if to say, "Make it stop." After two swishes of her tail, she sauntered back to her favorite spot to nap. Ten minutes later we repeated the entire procedure. After the rain stopped, Val no longer had any interest in going outside. She was content to snooze and to look out the window from her vantage point on the back of the sofa.

It is no fun to live life zigging when everything else is zagging.

A friend once told me that the secret to happiness is to choose what is already happening. Now, whatever transpires in my life, I say: "This is exactly the way I wanted it to be. Isn't it wonderful that everything has turned out this way."

It's hard to be in a bad mood when everything is precisely the way I want it. Do you think I can communicate this to Val?

Music to Our Ears

Roadside signs warn us of the fines for littering. Television reminds us of pollution's devastating effects on our environment and, ultimately, on us. We are repeatedly alerted to the deadly consequences of smoking, and now to the dangers from second-hand smoke. We are consistently bombarded with reminders of the adverse effects of our various assaults on Mother Nature.

I was recently reminded of a threat, however, that we have not yet come to regard as dangerous to our well-being. While out driving one afternoon, I noticed a car stopped at a traffic light. It was rocking from side to side, because the radio was so loud. It is time to raise our awareness of the effects of noise in our lives and to campaign against sound pollution and second-hand noise.

In ancient times, the "priest physician" was well acquainted with the dynamics of sound vibrations. The priest knew that persistent healing chants create vibrations that stimulate power centers, activating and releasing increased energy to all parts of the body, thus healing the form.

The sound vibrations we encounter every day either build up or tear down the body. We have a right to choose the sound vibrations that enter our personal space.

We All Need Attention

Next to my computer sits a beautiful pot of lush green ivy. Some of the plants in my house look uncommonly good, some don't look so good, and some need to be thrown out. However, the ivy that sits to my right is a superb specimen.

As I sit down to write every day, I look at this plant to see if it needs water, if the pot needs turning for a different angle of light, and if it could use some plant food. Sometimes I praise it for doing so well and looking so beautiful. Once in a while I even turn and ask its opinion about what I am writing.

People are like plants; they respond to attention. The ones who get the most attention are the ones who flourish.

Point of Power – Now

Things that are going to happen
begin now,
and things that don't happen
are things we intend to begin later.
Think about it—
even procrastination begins now.

There is More

"In spring a young man's fancy turns to love." How unfortunate to go through life thinking of love only in the terms of personal sentiment. Music, poetry, and philosophy proclaim that love is the greatest attribute we can express.

The truth is, love is all we are—and all that truly exists.

If we do not recognize love in every situation, it is only because we have constructed barriers against people, places, and things. Love rushes into every mind that releases resentments, perceived affronts, and the need to control. Love does not wait for perfect timing or perfect situations. Love waits only for an invitation. When self-constructed hindrances are released, love quickly floods into every situation.

When we walk in love, we walk in perfect peace.

> "Neither a lofty degree of intelligence, nor imagination, nor both together, go to the making of genius; Love, love, love, that is the soul of genius."
>
> Mozart

Heed the Alarm!

One morning at the retreat resort where I was staying, the fire alarm went off in the hall. When the clanging didn't stop after a few minutes, people began appearing. First, heads timidly extended from half-opened doors. Then, people ventured boldly into the hall in spite of their various stages of attire. Most of the responses to the continued, rhythmic screeches of the alarm were along the lines of "how to get the darn thing cut off." We eventually went back to our rooms to wait for building maintenance to rescue us from the noise. We never once considered that the alarm was a warning for our safekeeping!

This is a mirror of life: numerous warning signals sound to alert us that we are on the wrong path. Instead of heeding the alarms, we work out ways of overcoming or silencing them. When things don't work out, we look back and say, "I knew better; I had a feeling that things weren't going to turn out."

Warning signs that we interpret as stumbling blocks to success are only deterrents for our protection.

Give Me a Sign

I say, "God, give me a sign." The sign comes. Then I say, "God, give me a sign that this is the sign."

We don't trust the signs.
We don't trust ourselves.
We don't trust.

Instead, we have come to rely on outer appearances; however, these appearances are changing rapidly. We feel lost, and our society has become fragmented. Without trust in God's signs and in ourselves, we have nothing to build on. We find ourselves, our friends, and our neighbors living in fear. In this atmosphere, it is virtually impossible to establish a reality that feels secure.

It is time to take our focus off outer reality and to turn inward! If we can become still in moments of distress and rely on guidance from our Higher Power, we can begin a communication that will withstand the test of time and truth. This is a first step in establishing a new level of trust in our lives. When we are looking for a sign, guidance from our intuition is the sign that can be trusted.

Lighten the Load

Watching people move through life is similar to watching people maneuver on a moving sidewalk at an airport terminal. Usually, people prefer the moving sidewalk because of the heavy loads they are carrying. The excess baggage we insist on dragging along creates an obstacle course for everyone around us. We cannot move as fast as we would like because our superfluous baggage hinders balance and agility.

Cumbersome bulk has taken away many of our options. Along the way we get tired, so we stop for a breather, only to notice that our cumbersome luggage is blocking the progress of others. Every now and again, we get knocked about by the baggage hanging from someone who has moved alongside us. The passer-by usually fails to notice the discomfort that the baggage has caused us.

The less baggage that we carry with us from the past, the easier and swifter we are able to move through life. The less baggage we carry, the less chance we take of injuring others or of being injured by them.

It behooves us to look through our "stuff" and to discard what is no longer necessary, so that we can move along our pathway smoothly and effortlessly, at the pace we desire.

The Straitjacket of Comfort

Everyone has a favorite dish. Usually it is a "comfort food" that we associate with the nourishment of our body, mind, and spirit. It came into favor through pleasant memories and good associations.

Today, we are learning that some of our favorite foods are not good for the health of our hearts. Some of them clog our arteries and thus stifle life's flow.

This also holds true for many childhood associations that influence the choices we make today. Today's behavior comes from the favorite and comfortable ways that we found for doing things in the past. However, just as some of the ingredients of our "comfort foods" cut off life's flow through the body, many of the behaviors that feed our psyche clog life's flow and cause us to die to the fullness of life's possibilities.

Conscious Contact

We are all sparks from the Divine Flame. Our brilliance is created from the magnificence of Its presence. If we get too far from the Eternal Flame, we grow cold and die. If we remain near our source, we can re-kindle our power any time we feel our light growing dim.

Three in One

Most of us are striving for good health, but what is health? "Health," according to *Webster's New World Dictionary*, is "physical and mental well-being." Webster's also notes that "health" is derived from a word that means sound, hale, healed, and whole. In referring to the dictionary for the meanings of "healed," "whole," and "holy" — surprise! We find that they all mean the same thing. But, wholeness of what? Wholeness of spirit, mind, and body.

When we seek health, our thinking needs to include a concept of wholeness in body, mind, and spirit. True health will only be achieved if we embrace the principle that the quality of our health depends on the soundness of body, mind, and spirit — the three parts that make the whole.

> "A merry heart doeth good like a medicine: but a broken spirit dries up the bones."
>
> Proverbs 17:22

The Path

The "in" phrase today in spiritual circles is "on the path." In trying to find the "right" path, it's so easy to get preoccupied with reading the "right" books, attending the "right" workshops, and using the "right" jargon.

In the midst of all these "right" trappings of the spiritual journey, we have forgotten the magnificent simplicity of it all: we need only to bow our heads, to notice the rubbish we are standing in, and then to clear it away. Voila! There is the path. We have been standing on it all the while.

We each chose, in the beginning of time, a particular path so that we could learn our individual lessons. Each path is unique and holy, for all paths lead back to the awareness of our unity with God.

> " . . . put off your shoes from your feet, for the place on which you are standing is holy ground."
>
> Exodus 3:5

Take Time for Beauty

What are the keys to greatness?

Abraham Maslow, the developer of humanistic psychology, researched this subject for years. His discovery is both surprising and fascinating.

Maslow found that passion for truth, beauty, and virtue helped kindle the fire of creativity in the lives of great thinkers and achievers. He postulated that humankind needs to focus on such "secondary" drives. Truth, beauty, and virtue are the values that serve at the heart of the "self-actualized personality."

> "Beauty is truth, truth beauty, . . . that is all
> Ye know on earth, and all ye need to know."
>
> Keats

"These are Alma Two Boys"

I was browsing in an upscale used furniture store in L.A. when I spotted a photo album. As I opened it, an old photograph of two boys fell to the floor. When I picked up the picture I noticed on the back the handwritten, penciled inscription "these are Alma two boys, Wilmer and Richard, 1922."

The two young boys, who looked to be about seven and nine years of age, frowned into the camera. They were wearing high-top shoes, long stockings, knickers, and collarless shirts. Perched at rakish angles on their heads were spiffy-looking caps. The sunny side of a country frame house that had been built on brick supports stood in the background.

A rush of memories came flooding in, and I was filled with sweet sadness. For an instant I was swept back in time to my grandfather's farm house that held so many love-filled moments. The photograph reminded me of a picture I had seen of my father and his brother, Russell and Moncell. My father and Uncle Moncell are both dead. I wondered about Alma's boys, Wilmer and Richard.

Too soon my friends called, "Come on." I put the picture down, closed the album, and walked out onto the busy street.

It is good to pause and remember. Because of "Alma boys," a part of me that was dry and hard has been moistened and is soft again. Thank you, Wilmer and Richard.

Whose Reflection Am I Seeing?

As we grow in consciousness, what was once acceptable behavior becomes unacceptable. As we change, we affect everyone in the sphere of our influence. Our shift in consciousness filters into the community around us. Thus, as we grow and change, so does our community. It follows that the state of the nation is only a reflection of the current consciousness of the majority of the populace.

The people still have the power.

If we are disgruntled with what we see as trends in our community and in our nation, we must first recognize that these trends are merely reflections of consciousness. The only way to change a reflection is to change what is being reflected.

Don't Assume!

After conducting a funeral service recently, I was approached by a gentleman who told me how much he had enjoyed the service. He explained that he had understood my every word. He added that he had not grasped anything said during the many funeral services he had attended recently.

I began to puff up with pride with what I thought was this gentleman's apparent admiration of my ability to communicate ideas and feelings when so many others had failed. As he mused on, I drifted into thoughts about laudable phrases floating from my mouth. I was jerked back into reality when I heard him mention his new hearing aid and his success in finally finding one that worked for him.

I had no trouble hearing him when he enthusiastically exclaimed to me, " . . . and I was able to hear every word you said." I was reminded that we can't assume we know what people intend by the seemingly plain meaning of their words. For example, our perception of words as hurtful may be simply our misinterpretation of intent.

As a transplanted Southerner, I have become aware of a myriad of misinterpretations based on the differences in the manners and customs of the many different cultures in our own country.

The kind gentleman at the funeral that day gave me a new "hearing aid": don't jump to conclusions about intended meanings, give everyone the benefit of the doubt. A multitude of hurt feelings will be avoided.

Hopefully, my new hearing aid will work for me as well as the gentleman's worked for him.

Today Is the First Day of the Rest of Your Life

We always say, "Where has the time gone?" Today is a good time to look back on the past and to evaluate how we have been doing. Are we advancing toward our goals? Have we set goals to advance toward?

As for me, when I look back on my life, I realize that I have always tried to accomplish too much. I have spread myself so thin that I have not had the focus necessary to be a success in any one thing.

All of this is in the past however. Now I remember to begin every day with my new realizations: I am not the general manager of the universe, only the caretaker of my own soul, and that's responsibility enough. As I concentrate on being the best possible me—for just one day at a time—I ensure the best possible day in my life. Days turn into weeks, weeks into months, and then into years. The next thing I know, I have a lifetime of success to remember.

I Want a Big God

God informed us early on that we were created in God's image, but because of our insane egotism, we have projected our images onto God. This is an extreme case of the tail wagging the dog.

We look at ourselves and say, "Hey, God looks like me." If we're black, we think that God is black; if we're white, we think God is white; and so on through the rainbow. To make matters worse, we inject the whole masculine-feminine issue into the debate. In the name of God, we constantly bicker. Our ongoing theological debate about who's right and who's wrong creates much unnecessary turmoil.

All this does nothing more than set up scenarios that foster eternal disagreement. Amidst all the squabbling, it is difficult to establish a favorable climate in which to live the commandment "that you love one another as I have loved you." (John 15:12)

Maybe God is big enough for everyone to be right.

I Hear You!

We all want to be heard and understood. I do not mind if others don't agree with me, so long as I feel that they have taken the time and interest to listen and make some attempt to understand my point of view. Most often during conversation, we are so concerned with getting our own point across that we don't listen. We are busy forming our next statement, getting ready to spring into the conversation during the next pause.

Improper and inadequate communications are the main instigators of trouble in relationships. One of two things usually happens: either we feel that we are not getting our ideas across, or the other person feels that we are not understanding him/her. Either way, confusion and/or hurt feelings often result.

Today is a good day to begin concentrating on clear, concise communications. If we take responsibility for listening with the sole intent of understanding, an unexpected and wonderful thing happens: we begin to be understood in a new and refreshing way. As we give, so will we receive.

I Want Color in My Life

I love garden shops in the spring. As I look at the blanket of pink petunias, I ask, "Do these bloom all summer?" "Only if you keep the withered blooms picked off," replies the salesperson. Seems like too much trouble, so I walk away.

I tell another clerk that I am looking for something that blooms all summer, that is low maintenance, and drought and heat resistant, and that smells good. She rolls her eyes and walks away.

I believe that my expectations at the garden shop are a fairly accurate description of everything we would order for our lives if we could. We would like to have constant good times, without having to put forth much effort. We also want to be immune to hard times, to continue to flourish despite any depletion of resources.

Lives, like gardens, don't require hard work—just continuous, loving attention. Neglected lives, like neglected gardens, visibly show the result of lack of attention.

We can clean up our lives the same way we clean up our gardens. We begin where we are, cleaning around the area where we stand. We prune one outshoot and pull one weed at a time until all the rubbish is cleared away. When the weeding and pruning are ongoing, our blooms are continuous.

Embrace Your Uniqueness

My grown children have the same personalities that they had as babies when I brought them home from the hospital. Although they are siblings, they were, and are, distinctly different. Just as none of us has the same fingerprints, we all come into this life with different personalities and various agendas. Each of us has our own path, our own special destiny. That individual path can be found only by turning within and moving into the illumination of intuitive knowledge.

Because each person is unique, each path is unique; and because each path is unique, only one traveler knows and follows it. Still, we do not have to follow our respective paths alone. We have a trustworthy guide on this spiritual pilgrimage: our Higher Power. Although we have only one travelling companion, never fear. God is well-equipped to go the distance.

Do It Now

Procrastination! I have finally found a way out! When something needs doing—DO IT—DO IT NOW! Isn't that brilliant?

I've always had such good intentions. I've always been sincere in my aim to produce. I get hung up, however, on my precondition that I must finish the things on yesterday's list before I begin today's.

Imagine returning from a long vacation. Mail and newspapers are stacked high on the kitchen counter. We don't wait to open today's mail or to read today's paper until we've caught up the backlog. You can see where that would lead.

Begin with today—and sandwich in the past piece by piece. If we take care of this day—*now*—our tomorrows will take care of themselves, and our yesterdays will gradually fall in line.

"Behold, now is the acceptable time."
2 Corinthians 6:2

Inspired Decisions

Each of us, at one time or another, suffers from fear or anxiety about making a wise decision. Some of us even get caught in the irrational clutches of sheer panic. At these times, we frantically take long surveys from family, friends, and anyone else who will stand still long enough to hear our plight. Even if we find enough people to agree with our preferred choice, the anxiety may continue. This growing anxiety indicates that we have not found the appropriate answer.

When we make the correct decision, we know it from a sense of peace that engulfs us. True wisdom comes from what we call "spiritual knowing," which is a special combination of intellect, discernment, understanding, and awareness added to that magical ingredient called intuition. "Spiritual knowing" always transcends intellectual knowledge.

It behooves us to stop our frantic opinion surveys. This avid questioning is fruitless because from the world comes only worldly knowledge. During the next panic, turn within and seek the true wisdom or "spiritual knowing" that resides within. The lifting of fear and anxiety signals a sound decision that stems from intuition. Don't discard that next hunch; it may lead to the answer you have been seeking.

Don't Take Your Garbage to Work

One Monday morning I grabbed briefcase, purse, and lunch and dashed out of the house, eager to get to the office and begin my week. When I sat down at my desk and began to sort out everything, I discovered a blue plastic bag amid my pile of customary parcels. With curiosity I looked inside, only to see coffee grounds, toast scraps, and an empty milk carton—need I go on? I had brought my garbage to work.

More times than not, we take our psychological garbage to work. This is especially true on Mondays. At such times, it pays to be sure that any feelings of frustration, anger, or blame are attributed to the right "culprit" and not to some innocent bystander or unrelated circumstance that happens to be in the line of fire.

The rubbish which often seems to engulf us on Monday mornings may only be part of the weekend leftovers that should have been dumped in the garbage on the way out of the house.

Life Is Good

I remember watching my mother squish her hands into the cornbread dressing as she mixed in the drippings from the Thanksgiving turkey. Every rack in the oven was loaded with delicious-smelling casseroles. Mouthwatering pies on the buffet awaited the hand-whipped cream. Steam fogged the kitchen window against the chilled air of that Thanksgiving morning.

Years later, I scurried around my own kitchen putting the last-minute touches of red berries and golden leaves on the table as my daughter, Holly, stood on a stool and watched her "granny" squish and mix the cornbread dressing to perfection. We didn't need words to express the love that flowed through three generations of women as we prepared the annual Thanksgiving feast.

More years have passed; my mother is gone, and I have moved away. Holly calls long distance to find out if it is equal parts cornbread and light bread, and I can hear my granddaughter, Charlotte, laughing in the background. Immense love wells up in my heart.

It is gratifying to see the continuity of generations. After all, this is what life is about, and it is good.

God Always Says Yes

Have you ever had a craving that wouldn't go away? I have. One morning, when I was visiting my daughter in Paraguay, I woke up craving an avocado. I decided that my perfect lunch that day would be sliced pineapple and cottage cheese, a banana, and a large tree-ripened avocado. We had everything but the avocado.

I set out to procure the biggest, squishiest avocado I could find. From one fruit stand to another the reply I received was the same, "Sorry señora no agatata." How could this be? Avocadoes were the most plentiful fruit in that country, and they were in season. With each frustrating "no," my craving grew. When I looked at my watch I realized it was time to start for home. I was empty-handed and disappointed.

As I stood on the street corner not knowing where to look next, I exclaimed, "God, I wanted an avocado for lunch." To my great astonishment, an avocado hit me on the head and fell to my feet. I was standing under an avocado tree. I leaned over and picked up the avocado. It was plump, ripe, and the perfect size—exactly what I had wanted. As I headed home for lunch I said, "Thank you, God."

In my quest for the object of my longing, I had been guided to a place where my wish would be granted without cost to me. It was not exactly the path I had chosen, but a very successful avenue nonetheless.

Divine Guidance leads us to the fulfillment of our dreams even though it sometimes looks as if we are being led down a false trail. Have faith and trust in God.

If I Do, I Can Undo

Why is it that we don't want to take responsibility for what is happening in our lives? We are quick to point the accusing finger and absolve ourselves of cause and fault.

I thought about this when I was putting the laundry into the washer this morning. Do you remember when we were deluged with advertising about detergents that could remove that greasy "ring-around-the-collar"? We don't see those commercials anymore—maybe we wised up, figured that a good neck washing would prevent that "greasy ring," thus eliminating the need for any "super soaps."

When we clean up our act, the need for white-wash or cover-up diminishes, because the honesty of our intentions shines through, giving us a glow that radiates to everyone we meet.

It Ain't Over Yet!

I remember seeing a play called *It's Never Too Late*, about a middle-aged couple with grown children. This couple is dumbfounded by the pending arrival of a "bundle of joy." Not exactly what they had planned for their retirement years. By the end of the third act, we have come to know that this "little accident" has turned their lives around and brings excitement into a ho-hum existence.

When we overplan our lives, we don't leave space for excitement, adventure, or "little accidents." We want life to be safe, predictable, under control. Security has become our god. Being in control has become our preferred way of being.

In reality, nothing is permanent except change, which is the antithesis of security. So, looks like we need to loosen up! Life can be fun. It's never too late for anything if we let go and let God.

A Friend Is a Friend.

For months my manicurist, Jane, listened to me complain about and bemoan the actions of my friends. I told how insensitive and unkind they could sometimes be. The theme repeated itself over and over until one day when Jane put the nail polish down, looked up over her glasses at me, and said the most profound thing: "Maureene, do you call those people friends? They don't sound like friends to me. Friends are nice to you."

How had I missed the obvious? Friends don't have ulterior motives; friends don't point out your shortcomings every chance they get; friends don't play one-upmanship at your expense. Friends always have your best interest at heart.

Because most of us were raised in dysfunctional families, we developed distorted ideas of support and friendship. Consequently, we enter relationships that repeat patterns of past abuse. It is this that we call friendship.

Change the word "friendship" to "familiar" and we are closer to truth.

Lighten Up on Yourself!

Pick! Pick! Pick! Why are some people so picky? It doesn't matter what others do, or how well they do it; the faultfinders always have "just a little something" to add to make everything right.

These people have few friends. When they impose their perfectionism on others, as they always do, it gets old fast, and "frankly, my dear," it's not much fun.

The sad part is that perfectionists are a thousand times more critical of themselves than they are of others. Their lack of self-esteem makes them strive obsessively for an unreachable perfection. Because they are never completely satisfied with what they do, they always see themselves as failures.

Life is creative and constantly in the process of becoming. Because each moment makes the preceding one obsolete, perfection is possible only in stasis. In an ever-changing reality, each moment is complete, and stands alone in its perfection.

Running on Reserve

I came out of the grocery store late one night, climbed into my car, turned the key—and nothing happened. Running out of gas makes me feel so dumb. All that day, I had intended to stop for gas, but more pressing tasks took precedence. The result: I was stranded in a parking lot at night, feeling very foolish.

It's easy to let a busy schedule keep us from properly caring for ourselves. We sometimes push ourselves to a point where we can go no further: even our reserves have run dry.

Now, every morning before I begin my day, I give myself a "full service" check. If I am running on empty I take a moment to go into the Silence. There, I am filled with the Divine Power that is always available to me.

How long have you been running on your reserve?

Name It and Claim It

In Genesis 2:19, God gave Adam the power to name every living creature. By granting Adam the power to name, God has bestowed upon us the responsibility to name. Life is constantly bringing situations before us to see what we will name them.

A name is an arbitrary label that describes a mental image. By naming the people, places, things, and passages of events in our lives, we determine the nature of their development. Beings and circumstances have a way of becoming what we expect them to be. Repeatedly call a child clumsy, and the result will be a clumsy child. Call a marriage less than our hearts' desire, and that's where it stays. If we persistently tell ourselves that success is only a step away, success will continue to elude us because it will remain a step away.

We have the option to label any circumstance a disaster or an opportunity. It will develop accordingly. Whatever our decision is, God always says yes!

A Day to Remember

Celebrations are wonderful. I believe that rites of passage are celebrations that our society overlooks.

What day did I become a woman? Was it the day I put on lipstick for the first time? Was it the day my menses began? In more primitive cultures that first day as a woman would have been preordained, duly noted, and properly celebrated.

Recently, I participated in the rite of passage of my dear friend Brent, as he moved from student to Minister of God. We laughed as we remembered the beginning days. We cried as our souls connected with sublime happiness, for we realized that we were participating in a ritual with the Divine Force of the Universe.

Because of that day's importance, Brent and I tried to imprint each second of it on our memories. We looked forward to his new beginning as we celebrated a job well done. We knew that this was a precious moment, and we honored it.

Rites of passage are important to mark the special events in our lives. In celebrating them, we are assuring ourselves distinctive yesterdays to treasure. The events we focus our attention on today are the memories we etch into our future.

I Release You and Let You Go!

We are never prepared for the passing of a loved one. It seems harder when this loss comes suddenly and when life is finally at a satisfying peak. And yet as I write this, I can see that maybe this is the best time to go.

At such a difficult time, I am often asked, "Why?" Any answer I give cannot suffice, because human beings have not developed the capacity to perceive the complete picture and function outside our limited viewpoint. We are unable to look beyond our own individualities to see that we play—not a small—but a vital part in the intricate mosaic of time and space.

We can take comfort in the belief that the circumstances of a soul's leaving this plane of existence are, on some level, the result of a decision from a choice. God is Absolute Good. We are not left to the mercy of some cosmic throw of the dice.

We grieve, and we miss our loved ones. They have completed their task on this plane of time and have begun the next phase of eternal life. There is no death, there is only transition. Yes, we grieve, but we also bless our loved ones as they continue on life's journey!

Eye of the Beholder

What did the rat say when he saw the bat? "Look at the angel!"

We all experience life from our individual perceptions. In fact, that is how our separate realities are formed. We are each the hub of our universe, and everything we see is an out-picturing from our personal lenses.

If I look through happy eyes, life is good. If I look through greedy eyes, I never have enough. If I look through suspicious eyes, everyone is suspect. If I look through fearful eyes, any circumstance makes me fearful. Get the picture?

Our views of life and of people are only projections through our internal lenses. It's like a movie; if we don't like the picture, we don't attack the screen. We do something about what is being projected.

Planned Obsolescence

Although my computer is a very good one, the "Y" key stopped working the other day. When I called to inquire about having my keyboard repaired or replaced, I was told that it is obsolete and cannot be replaced. The gentleman added, "May I tell you about some of our newer models? They are so much faster." But why would I want a faster keyboard? My typing isn't that good.

With the growing population and the growing numbers of consumer goods that quickly become obsolete, our country is becoming as crowded as a junk pile. We live in a culture of planned obsolescence; unfortunately, the plan is beginning to crumble. We don't have enough space to dump the obsolescence.

We must rethink our values about durability and disposability. It's not as if some Saturday morning the entire country could have a garage sale. Who would buy?

Woman to Woman

We wanted the vote, we got it. We wanted equal rights, we got them. Now what? Now we learn to be the divine feminine we were created to be.

Women moving up the ladder of success expect themselves to emulate the masculine success pattern: It has been women's only model of achievement. Too many of us have forgotten that women have unique qualities to offer. It is now recognized that women approach problem-solving in a manner that is fundamentally different from that of men. Yet these feminine attributes have been regarded as inferior.

If we continue to devalue ourselves by imitating men, we will never mature into our potential. We will only continue to imitate male patterns. If we as women do not honor our feminine energy, created in God's image, how can we expect others to do so?

Realization in Mid-air

The other night I got out of my car, took a few steps and fell flat on my face. My daughter, who was visiting me, asked, "Mother, are you all right?" "Of course I'm not all right," I replied. "I'm lying here flat on my face."

My declaration was not exactly the truth, because in midair and on the way down, before my nose plowed up the wood chips, I was already thinking, "There's a Soul Food in this."

Every time we hit the dirt, every time we lose our footing, every time we miscalculate the distance, or every time we look foolish by falling flat on our face, we will be "all right" if we can remember that a spiritual lesson is right under our nose.

Positive Thinking

Every thought that we think creates a vibration that either builds up or tears down. Through its vibration, positive thought builds inner strength that establishes an environment for positive action.

It is natural to have challenges in life: little ones, big ones, strange ones, funny ones, unexpected ones, and even mysterious ones. When we have trained our thought patterns to expect good to come from each challenge, and to know that even in trying times the proper outcomes will transpire, then we have stacked the deck of life in our favor.

Life is sure to be easier if we refuse to dwell on what is wrong with our world and, instead, look for what is right.

I say to myself, "I expect good to come to me through every situation of my life!"

Keep On Keeping On!

When I was a child, my friends and I spent many of our Saturday mornings playing in a vacant lot. Sometimes we would find an old canning jar half-buried in some out-of-the-way place. If the jar had been there for a long time, its bottom would be covered by a layer of dried dirt. We discovered that if we filled the jar with water, the water would remain clear and clean because the dirt on the bottom was too caked and hardened to be disturbed; but that if we poured a steady, forceful stream of water into the jar, the dirt layer would soften, and the water would be dirty until all the dirt had been washed away.

I have come to realize that this jar-washing portrays what happened to me when I embarked on my spiritual journey, when I began to pour spiritual insight into my life's container. Spiritual energy stirs up all of our "stuff" as it eliminates anything and everything unlike itself. That is why, when we finally decide to change old behavior, things appear to get worse before they get better. When spiritual energy starts stirring up our mud, it is natural to feel as if we were better off before we started. Patience! This is a spiritual process of Divine Order.

Our Big Chance!

Because we cannot see over the walls of familiarity, it is difficult for us to determine when we are in a rut. The main trap—that keeps us in our rut—is not setting our goals high enough. By placing limits on our aspirations, we impose restrictions on what is possible.

Our world is changing so fast that the activities we considered impractical yesterday are totally within the realm of possibility today. Just look at the strange economy we are encountering. It is only an out-picturing of the shift and growth our world is experiencing.

In this time of change, we should look at the dreams and desires we put on the shelf yesterday, take them down and see them anew, as today's opportunities.

Now is the time to take a quantum leap from the rut of today's familiar onto the ground floor of tomorrow's possibilities.

Today is the opportunity of many lifetimes!

Hands-On Healing

We call doctoring the practice of medicine. We talk about the healing arts. However, it takes a lot of hands-on practice to turn anything into an art.

I grew up in a small town where everyone knew everything about everyone, and that included the town doctor. When Doc Sanders responded to a sick call, he already knew the medical history of each patient—and much more.

When I was ill, I would feel better the moment Doc Sanders walked through the door into my room. Sitting on the side of my bed, he would put his comforting hand on my arm as he felt for fever. While he looked me over with his perceptive eyes, he would say, "Maureene, can you tell me how it feels?" I knew that I had his total attention, and I would pour out my heart to him. He would assess the situation, give me a loving pat on the head, instruct my mother on the proper treatment, and go on to his next call.

Doc Sanders had perfected the art of healing.

Miss Clyde

Miss Hammock was an elderly lady who lived in a many-columned house with a wrap-around porch. She lived in only one room, and rented out the other, not only for the money, but also for the company. It was during World War II, and my father was away, so Mother and I were the fortunate ones to share this interesting lady's home. Even though I was only five years old, I remember this time vividly.

Every summer Miss Hammock's sister, Miss Clyde, a school teacher from Atlanta, came to visit. I loved Miss Clyde because she spent each summer throwing away everything Miss Hammock had collected during the preceding year as well as whittling away at the vast collection of treasures in the attic. I examined everything she threw out, and if I found anything to my liking, I took it back to our side of the house. I amassed what, as a five-year-old, I considered to be real treasures—old fountain pens, a jewel-encrusted earbob minus the mate, and postcards from the State capital. Actually, the real treasure was Miss Clyde. As the day of the big throwaway approached and my anticipation mounted, my watchful eyes constantly scanned her for the slightest hint of her outlandish attire that always signaled the arrival of that special day.

On that day, Miss Clyde would anchor her getup around two basic items: flared shorts and a halter-top. Scantily covering her freckled, ample body, they provided some relief from the sweltering summers of southwestern Georgia, in those days before air conditioning. With these basics, she always wore black patent leather, open-toed, sling-back, high-heeled pumps over old stockings, which she rolled down and tied below her knees. Her frizzy red hair would be pinned up off her neck and tucked into a multi-colored snood, which looked like a little hammock for her hair. She had crocheted it herself; crocheting was Miss Clyde's hobby. I can still see her standing on the side porch in all her regalia, readying herself for action as she slipped on white cotton gloves, carefully adjusting each finger.

With earbobs flashing in the sun and her bangle bracelets clinking, she added her very own finishing fashion touch that has instilled her in my memory as crystal-clear 50 years later as she was that day. She tied pages of newspaper around the bare portions of her legs and arms, as protection from the bomber-sized mosquitoes we native Blufftonians took for granted.

She was ready, standing there in all her glory—a knight armored for battle—a broom in hand and a look of determination in her eyes.

Where are the fashion individualists today? I miss you Miss Clyde!

"Physician, Heal Thyself"

Spirituality is many things to many people, for each pilgrim goes down a path different from every other. Thus, spirituality has no dogma.

In its multifacetedness, spirituality is universal. Its infinite number of paths have one purpose—to help one help one's self. Spirituality is for the individual: it provides us with a practical way of life that applies to the spiritual power available to each of us, every day of our lives.

Do you see that we've come full circle from the multifacetedness of spirituality to its universality to its multifacetedness again? I consider it to be a healing circle, for when enough of us live in peace, harmony, and unity within ourselves, a chain reaction will bring these qualities into the world. Look at it as adding weight to the LOVE side of the seesaw.

We assist in healing humanity by healing ourselves.

Protection

Weight loss has become a national obsession. One day I counted the television commercials for weight loss products. I also included the advertisements for various gadgets to get fleshy bodies into shape. By evening I realized that I had not included the commercials for the books, tapes, and hypnotic approaches to weight loss. (There is even a staple you can have placed in your ear that stops hunger when you pinch it.)

When food was not so plentiful in times long ago, a wife's plumpness was a sign of her husband's prosperity. This attitude was also a recognition that fullness of figure is protection for survival. I wonder: maybe we are unconsciously protecting ourselves with layers of fat from these times of anxiety, increased natural disasters, job insecurity, AIDS, and the threat of death and crime—from the uncertainty of our future in general.

We don't need those extra pounds for protection when we remember—"I am always protected by God's love."

Words! Words! Words!

Emerson was right when he said, "What you do speaks so loud I can't hear what you say."

When I think of how much energy we spend trying to present an impressive image for the approval of the people we are trying to affect, it makes me tired. We could channel all that energy into becoming the best people we can possibly be.

You see, I get suspicious when anyone tries too hard to convince me of something; it's a dead giveaway that they are only trying to convince themselves.

Truth needs no amplification. If we live our truth, it will broadcast from every pore and fiber of our being. Life gets very simple when we speak, act, and live the possibility of our finest selves.

Out of Mind, Out of Sight

Holly's large veranda, overlooking the tropical flowers in the garden, was a pleasant place to watch the sunset. Every afternoon during my visit with my daughter in South America, I sat in the same spot, contemplated the day, and enjoyed the cooler air that accompanied the setting of the sun.

Tom, a friend of my son-in-law, came into town on business during the second week of my visit. When Tom ventured out on the porch the first evening of his stay, I thought he had come to join me in the serenity of the stillness. Instead, he had come to inform me, "You can't sit out here this time of day; those mosquitoes will eat you alive." At that very moment, mosquitoes began to sing in my ears and I had to swat them off from my ankles.

To this day, I know that Tom called those mosquitoes to the veranda through his expectation of their presence. Because I had no experience with the insect life of this foreign country and thus no reason to expect discomfort, I had been able to enjoy a week of bliss in my special place. After Tom's arrival, I never sat outside again without looking for the mosquitoes, and they never disappointed me.

Because we create our reality from our thoughts and expectations, we always get what we expect. Interesting, isn't it? The old saying, "What you don't know won't hurt you," turns out to be true.

How Did I Get to be Me?

Why do I sometimes do the very thing that I said I would never do?

Could I be living my life unknowingly from the belief system of my parents and the philosophy of my childhood? Could my behavior be stemming from a subconscious filled with old and limited beliefs, beliefs that worked for me as a child but no longer serve my best interest? Whenever I take an honest look at myself, I find it helpful, and sometimes painful, because it takes a vast amount of courage and strength to question core values.

> "When I was a child I thought as a child, . . .
> when I was grown I put away childish things."
> 1 Corinthians 13:11

Increased capacity for living the full life is at our disposal when we are willing to become flexible. When we let go of attitudes that hamper our growth, it is possible to achieve our potential.

As Above – So Below

There is a universal metaphysical law known as the "law of vacuum": if we create a vacuum, nature fills it. Because this is a spiritual law, it works every time. Those circumstances in our lives that need changing must be cast out before the new can come in. Situations that need cleaning up have to be dealt with before we can begin anew. "Nature abhors a vacuum"; it always fills the vacant space. It is our job to provide a clean space to be filled.

If life seems stuck—get a bucket of soapy water, a brush, and find a place that needs cleaning. Do a good job of it and watch life clean up in a hurry. Start by cleaning out a desk drawer, organizing the garage, discarding the mountain of clothes you no longer wear. Whatever task you choose, do a good job of it, and watch your inner life clean up in a hurry.

When internal problems seem so messy that you don't know where to begin, begin at home. The order and condition of a person's house are always a reflection of the dwelling place of the soul.

Do Something!

When she became exasperated with me, Mother used to say, "I don't care if it's wrong; *do* something." Contrary to the way this sounds, there is much wisdom in these words. Without knowing it, my mother was unsticking me.

She was applying a law of physics known as the "law of inertia," which holds that the tendency of matter at rest is to remain at rest. The laws of physics govern us on all levels of our existence. When these laws extend beyond the physical into the mental and spiritual arenas, we call them metaphysical (more than physical) laws.

When we find ourselves feeling stymied, be it in a physical, mental, or spiritual dilemma, the important thing to do is to get moving. If we take one tiny step, it leads to another, which leads to yet another, and before we know it, our old momentum is back.

Slow Down

"The hurrieder I am the behinder I get." The more I allow myself to feel pressured, the more mistakes I make, and the faster the time seems to gallop toward my designated deadline. If only I could remember to stop, take a deep breath, and turn within.

When I turn within, time begins to slow to the point of stillness and I realize that time is merely humankind's limited consciousness of space. When I surrender to my Divine core which lives in this stillness, I free myself from the bondage of time. When I am operating from Divine space, I am in the space where time collapses and miracles happen. In this sacred space I am on "God's time," and there, all things are possible.

Millions Around Us

In the summer, one of my favorite things to do is to lie on the ground under a tree and look up through the leaves and branches into the heavens. Sooner or later, I begin to wonder how many leaves are on a particular branch. This inevitably leads to wondering how many leaves are on the entire tree. When I start to count the leaves I soon lose track, because of the sheer mass of foliage and the magnitude of the project. Then I ponder, "Is this what a million looks like?"

We live in a universe of plenty. God, through nature, provides more for us than we could possibly use. If you have ever had a garden or owned a fruit tree, you know what I mean. Nature is profuse in its generosity. It is our human condition that has created the idea of lack.

As I maintain an attitude of thankfulness for our world of plenty, I keep my focus on the abundance of good that God has provided us. If I temporarily forget the bounty that surrounds me, I need only to look again up through the foliage of a tree.

Seeing Clearly

Last week I discovered that I had been wearing my contact lenses backward for over a year. Of course, I immediately corrected my error. What a difference: now I can see! All along I had thought that even though I had paid good money for the lenses, not seeing well was the price I had to pay for my vanity and my desire to not wear glasses.

This is a paradigm of how life is sometimes. The way we see things stems from beliefs that we bought in good faith. Someone in our past sold us a bill of goods about ourselves and what we could expect in life, and we bought it. We have looked at life through these distorted beliefs and consequently what we see is a distorted reality.

It's a good idea every now and then to take out the beliefs that we have blindly accepted, examine them, and see if some adjustment is necessary. A change in viewpoint may bring about a clearer picture of reality.

Checkout Counter Blues

We are hungry for truth and beauty.

When we read the tabloids' headlines at the check-out counter, we wonder, "How can they top this one?" Next week it's the same song second verse: more ugliness, more scandal, more things that seem beyond our control.

I have a "new thought" affirmation that meets my check-out counter challenge: "I have limitless effects on every activity I am involved in. It is my duty and responsibility to take a stand for truth and beauty in all things."

When we adopt positions of integrity, the ripple effects of our words and actions not only have immediate impact but they reach into places that we have never seen. If we live our ideals consistently, we consciously become an active part of raising the consciousness of the planet.

I like the feeling of participating. The knowledge that I can have a positive effect on the world is empowering. Peace begins with me.

Things are beyond our control only when we give up and quit.

I Let Go of Control

"All in due time" is not music to the ears of those of us who like to be in control. One of the fundamental truths that we never seem to learn is that we can have everything if we are willing to do the groundwork and to allow Divine timing to play its part.

So many times I have thought I was ready, so I jumped in and "pushed the river" only to watch things screw up.

The Cosmic Christ within each of us has perfect timing through complete knowledge of the Cosmos. As we allow Divine timing into our lives, we begin to witness miracles in all our affairs.

When we surrender to our Higher Power, "Thy will be done" takes on a different ring; we begin to notice that all of our actions bring success and happiness. All details mesh as though they were being magnificently guided—and they are.

"All in due time" takes on a new meaning as we begin to realize that we can have it all—in God's time.

Expect Good

My daughter called last week, upset about the changes going on at her school. A creature of habit, like most of us, she is fine until a big shuffle of the deck is upcoming.

When we see change approaching, most of us tend to feel that we will be left out, that things will not go our way, or that we will end up with the short end of the stick. When the dust settles, however, we frequently find that all our worrying was for naught because everything has turned out fine and sometimes even better than expected.

We can't escape the reality that life is one big shuffle after another. As soon as we think that everything is in place, someone or something comes along and shuffles the deck. If we don't allow ourselves to expect good, we will live a life of constant worry, fear, and concern.

The key to happiness is to expect the best from every shuffle of the deck. Trust God and expect good.

I Don't Remember It That Way

The only access we have to our past is through memory. Yet despite our best intentions, memory is a slanted version of what happened. You could say that memory is selective. It may sound harsh, but the truth is that we remember only what is favorable to us.

When discussing a previous incident with a friend, we frequently have a difference of opinion about what had occurred. Our recall of any incident evolves from a few facts that are generously colored with creative bias. Using creative memory, we tend to recall a position that we presently want to promote. (All this is subconscious, of course.)

If we are building our future on a past that we remember with selective recall, we are building our future on fantasy, not fact.

God Wants Us to Be Happy!

Why can't I go into a department store without taking a "quick peek" in the children's department? Invariably I find something my grandchildren can't live without—to be more truthful, something Granny can't resist wanting them to have. Consequently, I do everything in my power to see that they get it.

The only way I can conceive of the depth of God's love for us is to imagine God as the "Super Granny." God does not wait for us to ask. She is constantly looking for ways to give us love. She is perpetually looking for wonderful gifts for us, gifts that we have not yet imagined.

She cannot resist bestowing her blessings on us. To receive this love, we have to do nothing but to turn to her. When we open our arms to her, she automatically sweeps us into her loving embrace. As she brings us to her bosom for comfort, she blankets us with love and peace.

A Time for New Wine

The discovery that the sun and stars do not revolve around the earth began the modern age. This new information altered the foundation for thought.

Einstein's theory of relativity and the uncertainty principles of quantum physics brought us the knowledge that what we perceive as solid matter is mostly space with energy patterns running through it. Modern scientific instruments enable us to study the action of these patterns, and we have learned that the act of observation affects the activity of the particles being observed. These observations also made it possible to establish the fact that the *expectations* of the observer altered sub-atomic particles. This new information marks the beginning of a new age. Again, we change the foundation for thinking.

Consider the profound possibilities implicit in this new foundation. One is that our expectations manipulate the energy that manifests itself as formed matter. How exhilarating! We really do get what we expect. It's a fact! This new information presents to us a "new thought" that cannot be contained in our "old thought" containers.

Maybe the reason why there is so much dysfunction in our society is that we are trying to force "new thought" into our old ways. It can't be done.

> " . . . new wine is put into fresh wineskins, and so both are preserved."
>
> Matthew 9:17

Universal Law of Mind Action

Like attracts like. Like begets like.
Thoughts held in mind produce after their kind.

I love the New Year! It's a time of new beginnings and clean slates. We say, "This time it will be different. This time I will get off the old merry-go-round and do things differently." Too often we think we've gotten off the merry-go-round only to find that we have merely changed horses—year after year, we keep riding the same old carousel.

True change doesn't come by altering the circumstances in our lives, for circumstances are only manifestations of our thoughts and beliefs. Thoughts are cause; and circumstances are effect. Real change comes only when we deal with the cause of unwanted circumstances—our thoughts.

When we change our perception about a situation, we begin to think differently about it, and the circumstance automatically changes. Change the cause and you change the effect. Thinking is cause.

Self-Portrait

I can look at my daughter Ellie's paintings and know that they were painted by her because she has a style that I call "pure Ellie." This "pure Ellie" doesn't follow the standard rules of art, yet Ellie's teachers consider her a successful artist because there is excitement in her originality.

When life is over, will anyone recognize your life's canvas from your unique style or brush strokes?

When faced with a blank canvas, most of us paint what we think the people most central to our lives want to see. As the primary characters in our lives change, we readily substitute a fresh palette and technique to fit the latest situation. Unfortunately, after years of trying to accommodate, we wind up with a canvas that is a hodgepodge of styles and colors—a canvas that says nothing.

Standing back, we can find a few portions of our life's self-portrait that are represented by authentic brush strokes that are "pure us." We might think "this part is good," or "I'm proud of this corner," or "wasn't my blending good there."

It takes courage to resist the urge to accommodate—and to be yourself. Being yourself, however, almost always means defying conventions. You see, we are each a true original, a unique creation of God. Only when we have the courage to be true to the Self we were created to be do we have any chance of becoming a masterpiece.

Cleopatra No More

I love country western music because it really tells it like it is. This morning I heard "You Can Call Me Cleopatra, Cause I'm The Queen of de-Nile." I chuckled as I turned up the volume.

It is difficult to address a problem if we refuse to admit that it exists. We go into denial for any number of reasons. When the many reasons are boiled down into one common denominator, however, it turns out to be our good old adversary—the ego. Whatever the problem, the ego always thinks that it knows best. The ego tricks, distorts, schemes, and maneuvers us so that it can maintain control. It is "the Queen of de-Nile."

Ego is the trickster, keeping us from the Divine Love that is always available when we surrender our narcissistic personalities to the Lord of our being. The millions who have found their way to health, happiness, and prosperity through "letting go and letting God" have relied on a prayer that we, kings and queens of denial, might try:

> "God grant me the Serenity to accept the things
> I cannot change, the courage to change things
> I can, and the wisdom to know the difference."
>
> The Serenity Prayer

Yin and Yang

God is spirit, neither masculine nor feminine. However, God embodies all the attributes of both yin and yang energy. If each of us is created in God's image, then what is our individual truth?

We are units of Divine Energy encased in a physical covering, which is expressing as masculine or feminine during this lifetime. The physical part of us has manifested on this planet solely for the spiritual development of each person's true self, which is neither masculine nor feminine, but is Divine Spirit.

How Does Your Garden Grow?

In the garden of my life what I sow, I reap. The seeds I sow are my feelings, my thoughts, and my actions. The crops I reap are the results of my feelings, my thoughts, and my actions. This makes me responsible for what keeps showing up on my plate.

When we get caught up in the emotional fallout from the unwanted events that keep appearing in our lives, we frequently forget that these circumstances are only the results of the seeds we sowed in our past. We forget that we can never separate effect from cause, as much as we would sometimes like to do. You see, we always reap what we sow. It's the law.

When we sow indiscriminately, the result of the harvest is a plate full of "goodies" that are sometimes hard to swallow.

Now, Be Nice

I have found a wonderful place for Chinese take-out. On my frequent trips there, I exchange smiles and courtesies with the man behind the counter. We have become friends of a sort. Once when I was paying for my meal, I reminded him not to forget my fortune cookie. "I'll give you two in case the first is not good," he replied, "but you don't seem like someone whose fortune is not good." I smiled and walked out to my car feeling sooooooo good.

It is easy to forget how important it is just to be pleasant, to give a compliment, or to exchange a smile. These are simple things that can make a big difference in someone's day.

Let us avoid consciously adding to any problem we come upon, and let's always endeavor to leave people, places, and things a little better because we were there.

"None of us lives to himself."
Romans 14:7

High Quality Life Ain't for Amateurs!

During my visit with a friend in Texas, we were browsing in a gift shop in the Hill Country when a sign on the wall caught my eye: "TEXAS AIN'T FOR AMATEURS." After my friend and I had a good laugh, I realized how true that claim is. I have known many a "professional" Texan. Serious Texans take great pride in their state.

From our easy chairs, we look with envy at the professionals who parade before us on our televisions, be they athletes, musicians, actors, or comedians. These professionals make a career of cultivating their skills, honing their talents to a level that highlights the differences between professionals and amateurs.

Anything we do with the energy and focus of a professional will produce a performance that is a source of pride.

One Little Step

Two years ago I joined a health club. As the manager was showing me around the gym, I noticed a young lady on a stair stepper. She had "itty-biddy" clothes on her "itty-biddy" firm body.

My tour of the gym took about thirty minutes and when we finished, the girl with the "itty-biddy" clothes and the "itty-biddy" firm body was still effortlessly stair stepping. She had not even worked up a sweat.

In my size large sweats, I walked confidently over to the stair stepper, took five agonizing steps, humbly stepped down, walked out the door of the gym, and never went back. I paid my dues to the gym for a year, but that was as close to exercising as I could get.

There is a moral to this story. That day two years ago, if I had done my five steps on the stair stepper and if the next day I had returned to do eight and so on, today I would be the lady in the "itty-biddy" clothes with an "itty-biddy" firm body.

It is hard not to fall into the clutches of our "instant success" society. In this day of instant coffee and gourmet microwave meals, we have been conditioned to want everything yesterday.

I need to remember that all things are achieved one step at a time.

Part of the Whole

Teilhard de Chardin often pointed out the "unimpeachable wholeness of the universe." What does this mean to us in our personal everyday life?

It means that, as a part of the universe and its wholeness, we are each included in its soundness, integrity, and perfection. It means that we do not walk our paths alone; even if we take many wrong turns we can finish at the right destination, for we are guided by a power that knows more than we.

We will always end up where we need to be if we let ourselves be guided by the Truth of the Universe. It is infallible: it is God.

Who's Mama Now?

As a young boy put a bag of cookies into his mother's grocery cart, I overheard her say to him, "Do you think you deserve that?"

Unfortunately this well-meaning mother didn't realize the possible negative effects her nonaffirming message might have on her son's future self-worth. Statements like "Who do you think you are," "You'll never amount to anything," and "You're so bad" plant seeds of negative self image, and self-worth and inadequacy that continue to bear fruit for many years. In the actions of a student, husband or wife, mother or father, employee or employer we get to observe the ripple effect of a self-image implanted in our formative period.

The responses that we make as adults to many of the conflicts that we encounter come directly from those same self-images of ourselves that we subconsciously acquired as children—from the ones whom we thought loved us the most.

Rome Wasn't Built in a Day

Finally, in my hands, I held my manuscript. Even though it wasn't the finished product, it was bound, it was thick, and it had my name on the cover. As I flipped through the pages of my first book, what flashed through my mind surprised even me—"So this is how to write a book, one word at a time."

Because the finished product is the only "out-picturing" we novices have of any new undertaking, we have a tendency to become overwhelmed. When beginning the new project we forget that a mountain is climbed one step at a time, that a fortune accumulates one penny at a time, and that weight is lost one pound at a time.

Every project, no matter its magnitude, is accomplished one step at a time. Every life is lived one moment at a time, and every philosophy is conceived one thought at a time.

Love Me Dearly

I love me! I love me! I love me!

Can I say this without cringing? If not, then I have to question my ability to love you. Because you are only a reflection of me, it is true that if I don't know how to love myself, then I don't know how to love you. My expectations of you are only a projection of the expectations I place on myself. The ways that I treat my family, friends, and mate are a mirror of the ways I treat myself. What I think of others accurately mirrors my present concept or picture that I have of myself.

Although these attitudes and actions toward others are not calculated on our part, they automatically exhibit because we can only give out what we possess within. So, if our desire is to give love freely, then the question we must ask is, "How do I love me?" Let me count the ways.

Don't Take It to the Limit

The speedometer on my car says that it will go 140 miles per hour. Maybe it will and maybe it won't. I haven't pushed it to the limit, so I don't know.

Most of us live in the fast lane of life, pushing ourselves to the limit. We try to use all the technology of the day to cram maximum productivity into every second. For example, while grocery shopping one afternoon, I overheard a strange conversation in the produce section. I turned around to see a woman sacking tomatoes as she used her cellular phone to schedule a doctor's appointment.

Just because my car can supposedly go 140 miles per hour doesn't mean I have to take it to the limit. We all need some down time—precious time to refuel our energy supply. Today, conservation of energy is important in more ways than one.

It's no fun to run out of gas in heavy traffic.

"Be still and know that I am God."
Psalms 46:10

Pray Believing

Do you have trouble accepting good things in your life? Do you find that you pray, but you don't believe that your prayers will be answered? Do you secretly believe that your desires and actions are not worthy of approval from the Divine Power?

All that is God's is ours by divine inheritance, for we are the children of God, made in God's likeness and image.

Prayer is not supplication, but an affirmation of Truth—Truth that may not yet have entered our conscious awareness. When we are capable of accepting that good, it will be ours automatically. So, we pray believing that it is ours, and it is. God answers our prayers according to our expectations, because God always says yes.

"'And whatsoever you ask in prayer,
you will receive, if you have faith.'"
Matthew 21:22

One Day at a Time

Each day is precious and important. During each day we have many moments of adversity and unpleasantness, as well as many moments of joy.

As architects of our lives we determine those moments that become the building blocks of our life's foundation. Moments of focus become the environment of memory. We choose our building blocks every day, for we are constructing our lives one day at a time. Because each day is filled with happy as well as sad moments, we can find something to enjoy even on the "worst" of days. If we choose to dwell on the joyful moments, we assure a life of fullness, built upon a sound quake-proof footing.

Each of us has a choice: concentrate on the quality moments and build a life of contentment, or the crumbling moments, and allow misery and discontent to enter. How sad it would be to let our days slip by unnoticed until, one by one, we have frittered them away. Time cannot be reclaimed or relived. This is why the saddest words are, "If only I had . . .". You fill in the blank.

Put Away Childish Things

Whenever any "people" situation gets weary and ridiculous, it is time to call forth our sense of humor—a smattering of imagination wouldn't hurt either—and try the following exercise: In the midst of the bickering and squabbling, imagine the cast of characters in this drama as children. Visualize each person wearing a costume appropriate for the personality and juvenile age he or she is exhibiting at the moment. Quite a sight, isn't it?

After a few minutes of this, we can easily assess the maturity levels from which everyone has been functioning. In severe levels of stress and conflicts, a person functions at the age level where he/she got stuck during the developmental process.

This imaginative interpretation helps us understand why mature ideas can be difficult to bring into realization. With this understanding, we can defuse our feelings of being intentionally misunderstood.

> "You ought not to practice childish ways, since you are no longer that age."
>
> Homer

Oh! What to Do?

Because of decisions I have bungled in the past, I don't like to take responsibility for the ones coming up. I prefer to take advice from anyone and everyone rather than depend upon my own counsel. Being able to say, "They told me to do it," is good insurance against taking the blame for a decision gone wrong.

The problem with relying upon the advice of others is that each of us is taking a different life's test. The right answer for one person is usually not right for another.

In the past I created much chaos in my life by trying to cope with the challenges of my life's test with someone else's answers. I would not have bumbled so many decisions had I relied on my own counsel and followed my own instincts.

Okay . . .
So we don't live by bread alone—
a piece of pie or a little something sweet
with a cup of coffee couldn't hurt!

Ernestine's Sweet Potato Pie

2 eggs (beaten)
1-1/2 cups of sugar
2 cans sweet potatoes, drained (16 oz.)
1 can of evaporated milk
1/2 cup of butter (melted)
1 tsp. vanilla
1 Tablespoon cinnamon
1/2 tsp. nutmeg
1 cup chopped pecans
1 9-inch unbaked pie shell

Mix all ingredients well; if it needs any more of anything, add it. Pour into unbaked pie shell. Bake at 425 degrees for 15 minutes, reduce heat to 350 degrees and cook till firm.

Aunt Laura's Bread and Butter Pudding

12 slices Texas-style bread (thick)
soft butter
5 whole eggs
4 egg yolks
1-1/4 cups sugar
1/8 teaspoon salt
4 cups milk (4% milk fat)
1 cup heavy cream
2 teaspoons vanilla
powdered sugar (for topping)
fresh fruit

Butter each slice of thick bread. Combine and beat eggs, yolks, sugar and salt. In sauce pan, combine milk and cream—scald. Gradually blend heated milk into egg mixture. Add vanilla last.

Place slices of bread in pan buttered side up. Pour custard over bread and cook in preheated oven 375 degrees for about 45 minutes, or until knife comes out clean. Sprinkle generously with powdered sugar and glaze under hot broiler. Serve topped with pureed fresh fruit. I like raspberries, but strawberries are good too.

Lip Smacking Good Apple Pie

6 medium sized cooking apples
1 teaspoon cinnamon
or (1 can apple pie filling+1 teaspoon cinnamon)
1 10-inch unbaked pastry shell (deep)
1 cup sugar
1 cup graham cracker crumbs
1/2 cup flour
1/2 cup chopped walnuts
1 teaspoon cinnamon
1/4 teaspoon salt
1/2 cup (1/4 pound) butter
1/2 pint (1 cup) whipped cream
1 teaspoon cinnamon

Pare, quarter, core and slice apples; arrange in unbaked pastry shell. Sprinkle with 1 teaspoon cinnamon (or mix cinnamon and pie filling and pour in unbaked pastry shell). Mix together sugar, graham cracker crumbs, flour, nutmeats, cinnamon, and salt; sprinkle over apples. Melt butter and pour evenly over topping. Bake for 1 hour in a moderate oven 350 degrees, or until apples are tender.

Serve at room temperature. Whip cinnamon into cream until cream is stiff and place a dollop on each serving piece.

Pears a la Mrs. White

4 ripe pears
2 Tablespoons lemon juice
3 cups apple juice
1 cup sugar
1 or 2 (4 inch) cinnamon stick(s)
4 thinly sliced lemon slices
6 whole cloves
lemon rind strips (optional)

Peel, half and core pears. Brush pears with lemon juice to prevent browning. Combine other ingredients in a Dutch oven; bring to boil. Place pears in mixture, cover and reduce heat, simmer 15 to 20 minutes or until tender. Let pears cool in mixture and remove. Cook liquid until syrup consistency.

Serve cool or warm on dessert plate in pear syrup. Garnish with lemon slices and clove. Pass warm thick cream as a topper.

Vinegar Pie

(My children's favorite)

4 eggs (beaten)
1-1/2 cups sugar
1 stick butter (melted)
1 Tablespoon corn meal
2 Tablespoons flour
3 Tablespoons cider vinegar
1 Tablespoon vanilla
1 9-inch unbaked pie shell

Preheat oven 350 degrees. In large mixing bowl, combine all ingredients and mix well. If not sour enough, add 1 more tablespoon vinegar. Pour into pie shell and bake until firm, about 45 minutes. Cool before serving. Top with sour cream and chopped nuts.

Heavenly Hash (or, Yum-Yum)

2 cups crushed pineapple
1 lemon (juiced)
3/4 cup sugar
2 Tablespoons plain gelatin
1/2 cup cold water
3/4 cup grated sharp cheese
1/2 pint stiffly beaten cream
1/2 cup mayonnaise
1 cup cherries
1 cup chopped nuts (pecans)

Heat 2 cups of grated pineapple, add the juice of one lemon, and sugar. Stir until sugar dissolves. Soak gelatin in cold water 10 minutes. Add to hot mixture. Cool until it begins to set. Add grated cheese, whipped cream, mayonnaise, cherries, and nuts. Refrigerate until set.

Cut into squares and serve as a fruit salad or scoop into compotes as dessert. It's yum yum.

Georgia Cracker Pie

20 saltine or Ritz crackers (crushed)
1 cup sugar (divided)
2 teaspoons baking powder
3 egg whites
1/2 cup chopped walnuts
1 teaspoon vanilla

Preheat oven to 320 degrees. Combine crushed crackers, one-half cup sugar, and walnuts; set aside. Beat egg whites until stiff; add sugar and baking powder gradually. Fold cracker mixture into egg white mixture. Pour into greased nine-inch glass pie plate. Bake for 1 hour or until knife comes out clean. Cool before cutting. Serve with whipped cream.

Jellied Pecans

1 Tablespoon gelatin
1/4 cup cold water
1/4 cup boiling water
1/2 cup sugar
1/2 cup sherry (sweet)
1/2 cup orange juice
2 Tablespoons lemon juice
1-1/2 cups pecan pieces

For 5 minutes let gelatin stand in cold water. Add boiling water and stir until dissolved. Stir in orange juice, lemon juice, and sugar, blending well. After mixture has cooled slightly, add sherry. Cover bottom of square shallow pan with half of the mixture. Place in refrigerator. When chilled portion is nearly set, cover with pecan pieces, then cover with remaining jelly. Chill until firm. Cut into squares and top with mounds of whipped cream.

Aunt Irene's Date Nut Cake

4 eggs
2 teaspoons vanilla
1 cup sugar
1 cup self-rising flour
1 16 oz. package dates, chopped
4 cups chopped nuts

Preheat oven to 300 degrees. Beat eggs, vanilla, and sugar. Toss flour, dates, and nuts; add to egg mixture. Pour into a greased and floured tube pan. Cook about 1 hour 15 or 20 minutes; very slow oven may take longer. Cool 30 minutes before removing from pan. May be served with whipped cream.

Better than Sex Cake

(Prepare to swoon)

1 box Duncan Hines butter cake mix
1(8 oz.) pkg. chocolate chips (sweet)
1 (8 oz.) pkg. pecans, chopped
1 box instant French vanilla pudding
1/2 box German's chocolate (unsweetened), grated
1 (8 oz.) carton sour cream
1/2 cup cooking oil
1/2 cup sweet milk
4 eggs
1 stick butter

Icing:
1 (8 oz.) pkg. cream cheese (room temperature)
1 box confectioner's sugar
1 tsp. vanilla
Nuts and coconut (optional)

Mix all ingredients into cake mix. Pour into greased and floured tube or Bunt pan; bake 1 hour at 350 degrees or until done.

(Stick broom straw into cake, if it comes out clean cake is done.)

Icing: Cream the cheese and sugar until smooth; add vanilla, nuts and coconut. Spread over top of cake.

For a Happy Life

2 heaping cups of patience
2 handfuls of generosity
1 heart full of love
1 head full of understanding
***splash generously with laughter

Sprinkle in ample portions of kindness; add a good measure of faith. Mix well. Spread generously over a lifetime and serve to everyone you meet.

ORDER FORM FOR TAPES AND BOOKS

Please send me ______ copies of the book *Soul Food*.

I am enclosing a check or money order made out to Valhalla Press for $9.95 per book plus $2.00 handling for the first copy and $1.00 for each additional copy.

California residents add 7.25% sales tax.

AUDIO TAPE ORDER

Please send me the following tapes which are unedited recordings of talks by Maureene Bass. Each one has a guided meditation on the reverse side.

NO. OF COPIES

A ______ The Lord's Prayer-Revisited-part 1
B ______ The Lord's Prayer- Revisited-part 2
C ______ Starting Over
D ______ What Enthusiasm Can Do for You
E ______ The Holy Heart
F ______ The Cosmic Power is Our Power
G ______ Cause and Effect
H ______ Love
I ______ Friends
J ______ Good and Evil
K ______ Meditation
L ______ Relationships
M ______ Surrender
N ______ Living in the Now
O ______ Personal Powerlessness
P ______ I Am (the source of my power)
Q ______ How Divine Energy Works
R ______ True Prayer
S ______ Universal Law

T ______ Basic Laws of the Mind
U ______ Soul Food Stories

I am enclosing $8.95 per tape. Postage and handling for the first tape is $1.50 and .75 for each additional tape.

Please make check or money order payable to:

Valhalla Press

P.O. Box 6224

Napa Valley, CA. 94581

WORKSHOPS AND SEMINARS

MAUREENE BASS is a well-known speaker, teacher and minister in the San Francisco Bay Area. Maureene is available to speak or to teach in your area by special arrangement. For information regarding workshops and/or lectures write to:

P.O. Box 6224, Napa Valley, CA. 94581.